The Journey of Praying Frog

By Marc Zirogiannis

Zirogiannis, Marc
The Journey of Praying Frog

 33 pages

ISBN#: 978-1-312-47804-6

Inquiries or additional information contact:

Marc A. Zirogiannis
57 Ira Road-ste 114
Syosset, NY 11791
Email: mmasuperstore@gmail.com

Or visit

www.lulu.com

PRINTED IN THE UNITED STATES OF AMERICA

FOR SORAYA

THIS BOOK IS DEDICATED TO
MASTER EDWARD PARK

About the Author

Marc Zirogiannis holds a B.A. from Long Island University and a *Juris Doctor* from Hofstra University's School of Law. Mr. Zirogiannis is a world renowned Business Development Consultant. Mr. Zirogiannis has practiced the martial arts for over 25 years and earned a 2n^d Dan under the supervision of Grandmaster Yeon Hwan Park in Levittown, New York. He has been active in meditation for, over 10 years. He is a Taekwondo Referee with 25 years of experience. He has published numerous books on a variety of subjects, and, is currently the lead correspondent for an international Tae Kwon Do print publication. He lectures on a variety of topics, including suicide prevention, business development, and matters of the martial arts. His last novella, **Hitler's Orphan: Demetri of Kalavryta,** has won critical acclaim and been the subject of a radio program. It is currently in negotations to become the basis of a more extensive work.

Acknowledgements

Special gratitude goes to the entire Y.H. Park family for their love, support, and guidance, for over 25 years. This book is dedicated to Master Edward Park, of the **Y.H. Park Taekwondo Academy**, in Levittown, NY for his commitment to the physical, mental, and personal development of children. For such a young man he has the wisdom of many lifetimes.

Frogs have a special place in my home and that is why they place such a prominent role in this work.

The Praying Frog comes from my dear cousin, Lisa Bakker, and for that I thank her.

-Marc Zirogiannis

Figure 1-The Praying Frog

The Wisdom of the Fly

Praying Frog sat on the lily pad contemplating the universe. His legs were crossed, of course. His small hands folded in his lap, one of the four fingers on each hand slightly touching. His eyes were closed but he was awake and aware.

As he sat motionless a large, hairy, black fly buzzed about his head. He could easily have snatched him with his long tongue, but should he? After all, it was his nature. But did it have to be? Was there a different path for this enlightened amphibian to take?

Just as Praying Frog decided that his hunger had left him no choice but to eat the hovering menace, the Fly spoke.

"Wait", he said, shocking Praying Frog with his ability to speak.

"A talking fly?" he thought to himself.

"Of course I can talk," the Fly uttered, reading Praying Frog's thoughts. "Are you so arrogant as to think that only frogs have the gift of speech?"

"No" said Praying Frog. "I just never considered the possibility".

"Before you eat me can I ask you an important question"?

"A question? Okay, go ahead," he uttered, as Fly circled about, in his view, almost daring him to strike.

"What is your purpose, Praying Frog?"

"What do you mean?   What are you talking about?"

"What purpose do you serve?   Everyone and everything must have a purpose for their life, or your life has no meaning, whatsoever. This is a basic premise that gives meaning, even to the life of a lowly frog."

"I don't know my purpose. This, too, I never considered. I don't think I ever thought about what my purpose was," Praying Frog said in a dejected manner. "You ask as if you have some knowledge of the answer. Do you know my purpose?"

"I do," said the Fly.

"Will you share it with me?"

"I can," said the Fly, "but only if you promise not to eat me."

"I promise," said Praying Frog. "You are safe in my presence. Please tell me my purpose. I must know my purpose".

"Okay," said the Fly. "Just give me a second. I feel so tired. I need to take a short rest." Just then the old fly landed on the head of Praying Frog. Being already seven (7) days old, the Fly closed his eyes and fell into the eternal sleep.

"Oh no" thought Praying Frog. "Now I am, surely, doomed to live a life with no purpose at all!"

Amphibious Panic

Praying Frog found himself overcome with a sense of loss and panic. Why? What had changed? He was the same frog he had been moments prior to the Fly's visit, yet he felt, entirely, different. He was now a frog with no sense of purpose.

Praying Frog tried to compose himself. "My life is good and complete," he thought to himself. "So what if I have no sense of purpose." He thought the words to himself, but he did not believe them. He knew that the Fly had uncovered a glaring deficit in his life. In fact, the Fly had revealed that he wasn't really living at all, just taking up space.

He sat for a time thinking about his entire life, from Tadpole to maturity. He thought about his parents and his kids. He thought about his army and his home. All of those things felt like lies now. Without purpose, what was his life all about?

Where would he find the purpose for his life? Where could he uncover the answer he sought? Where could he learn his purpose so that he could return to living, again, instead of obsessing about this question? It was then he remembered that the Frog Library contained hundreds, maybe even thousands, of great books. "At least one of them should help me find my purpose." Of course, that was the place he needed to go.

He hopped quickly to the library and poured through the

greatest Frog works of history and philosophy ever recorded in writing. Amongst these classics of literature and history there must be something written that explained his unique purpose.

Praying Frog began his scholarly work. He studied and studied. He read and he read. He pondered and he queried amidst the mountain of books at the Frog Library. He discovered so much about the world he lived in. He learned about the physiology of frogs. He learned about the history of frogs. He learned about the psychology of frogs. He learned just about everything there was to know about frogs. There was so much to read and so much to learn and understand. He absorbed so much information, in so many academic and philosophical areas, but the one he sought.

After several hours of researching, Praying Frog found himself dozing off into an open book about the theology of frogs. As he fell into a deep, sound, sleep his mind, undoubtedly, was richer for all the knowledge he had received; however, he still knew nothing of his purpose, except that it was nonexistent.

The Dream

Deep in his sleep, Praying Frog began to dream. In his sleep he wandered the vast, blue planet in search of his purpose. In this vision, he was an older, broken down, lonely version of himself. He was tired and feeble from the burden of the journey, but he marched on, singularly focused on finding his purpose.

As he hopped over a rotted log he came upon a large cave in the distance. On the outside of the cave he could detect the outline of a sign, which his failing eyes could not make out the writing on from a distance. He hopped closer and closer until he could, clearly, see the words carved into the sign. They read,

"PRAYING FROG-IN THIS CAVE YOU WILL FIND YOUR TRUE PURPOSE ".

He was filled with emotion, anxiety, and excitement. His lifelong journey was about to have meaning. He had given up everything for the promise of the moment when his true purpose would be revealed to him.

Praying Frog gathered his composure, and then moved towards the cave. As he approached the cave he, suddenly, fell into an eternal sleep, as the Fly had done, before his eyes, leaving him to have breathed his final breath without ever learning his life's true purpose.

Praying Frog awoke in a terrible panic. "What a terrible nightmare," he thought. It had seemed so real. He knew that he must find his purpose in life before it was too late.

12

Frog Family Reckoning

Praying Frog gathered his frog family at their common lily pad. Present at the gathering was his frog-mate, Raya, and his 4 beloved frog-sons, DJ, Deme, Jojo and Bashie. These offspring were all the frogs that had survived from the thousands of eggs that he and Raya had fertilized together. While that was sad, it was a natural part of the existence of a common frog. They were thankful for the ones that had survived, and tried to protect them every chance they got. DJ and Deme were fully developed frog-lings, while Jojo and Bashie were still, merely, tadpoles.

"Family, I have gathered you together to tell you something very important. I will be leaving you today for an important journey," Praying Frog informed them.

"What, Daddy?" Sebastian, his youngest asked. "Where will you go? When will you be back?"

"I do not know how long I will be gone. I would never leave you if it was not so important."

"What is so important that you would leave us, Dad?" his eldest asked.

"I am going on a journey to find my purpose."

"Purpose?" Jojo asked. "What is a purpose, Daddy?"

"Our purpose is what we are supposed to do with our lives. It is what gives our lives value and meaning. Once we know our purpose, then we can start to behave properly to fulfill that purpose."

"Oh," said Deme, not really understanding what Praying Frog was talking about.

"More important than what our purpose is, is the matter of what it is not. In other words, without purpose we are just living empty lives, with no value or meaning. Just taking up space in this world, without contributing anything. Until I find my purpose I can't be a good father, or a good husband, or a good citizen, or have a good life. Once I discover my true purpose all of that will change forever. It will be worth the sacrifice."

"Where will you seek this purpose?" asked his eldest.

"I am going first to he *Council of Toads*, many ponds from here, across the marsh. The Council is made up of wise, old toads that are rumored to have the answers to many of life's important questions. Hopefully, once I get there they will reveal my true purpose to me and then we can start living better lives."

"We love you, Daddy, even if you have no purpose. Please be safe. Please come home soon."

He kissed his wife and his sons, one by one, on their little, frog heads, and then headed out for the *Council of Toads* with excitement and, a little, trepidation.

The Close Call

Praying Frog set out for the *Council of Toads*. While he didn't know exactly where the Council was located, he did know it was well beyond his familial pond and well past the nearest marsh. So, it was in that direction, he ventured.

Time had escaped Praying Frog as he journeyed on. It seemed liked days of traveling to Praying Frog, but it was, in reality, only a few hours that had passed. He hopped and hopped, thinking about how much better his life would be once he found his purpose. The odd thing about it was that he thought his life was pretty good before the Fly entered it and made him realize that he was living a purposeless existence. How could he have been so foolish and delusional?

While Praying Frog was busy contemplating his state and venturing farther and farther away from his home, he lost track of the fact that he was getting further and further from any water source. He was so deep in thought about how it is he could have lived so much of his life without any purpose that it wasn't until his, normally, moist, slimy skin began to feel dry that he began to be conscious of the true danger he was in. For Praying Frog's species of frog moisture was essential to life. Without nutrient rich, clean, water he would, surely, wither and die rather quickly.

Once Praying Frog became aware of his drying state, this condition became the focus of his thoughts. He was concerned, at first, but not yet panicked. He was a resourceful frog and thought he would figure it out. There had to be some water source nearby. A puddle. A pond. A stream. Perhaps, even a moist leaf or wet rock basin. Sadly, there was no such water source in Praying Frog's path.

He began to grow weaker and weaker. He became slower and more listless. "The *Council of Toads* can't be too far ahead now," he hoped. "The Council convenes in a wet, marshy area," he thought to himself. "I will be safe once I get there," he thought out loud.

The more he contemplated his dilemma, the more he recognized that he had never, actually, been this far from home. He had spent his entire life among his army of frogs, in the pond that was his home. "Maybe this wasn't such a smart idea," he thought for a moment. He then quickly erased the negative thought from his mind. "No, it is better to have died in pursuit of my purpose in life then to go on living a long life with no purpose at all."

Death, in pursuit of his purpose, was a real possibility at this point. Praying Frog was growing dryer, weaker, and more tired. He stopped hopping to conserve his energy. There was no marsh or pond in sight. It looked like this, really, would be the end for him. His mind began to slow, as his body had done, previously, and he began to accept his eternal fate as the miraculous first drops of cool, refreshing rain landed on his dry, scaly back.

The pure, cool rainwater was, immediately, absorbed through his porous skin, refreshing, invigorating, and saving the life of Praying Frog. He felt himself being awakened in body and in spirit and he began, quickly and gleefully, hopping towards the Council. "I will live to discover my purpose," he assured himself.

After just a short distance from the start of the rain he came upon a large marsh, where the signage read, "*THE COUNCIL OF TOADS*".

The Council of Toads

The five, lumpy headed toads sat in a semi-circle, awaiting frogs from throughout the surrounding marshes and ponds, like Praying Frog, to approach them, in search of their guidance.

The Council members were kindly, wise, and mature. They took their roles as elder statesmen and scholars very seriously. They were rumored, together, to have all of the knowledge of the modern and ancient world at their disposal. There was nothing, allegedly, that they did not know about.

"What brings you before the great *Council of Toads*, common frog?" the center seated Toad inquired.

"I am Praying Frog, from the Green Lily Pond, and I have come seeking the wisdom of the Council."

"Very well. Ask your question, Praying Frog," one of the Toads on the Council requested.

"I have come to ask your esteemed panel what my purpose is in life," Praying Frog asked the Council.

"Your purpose?" one of the Toads asked. "Whatever do you mean?"

"My purpose, wise sirs. I have come to ask you what my unique, purpose in life is so that I may live a happy and productive life in fulfillment of that purpose."

"What makes you think you have a purpose?" another of the Toads inquired.

"Everything and everyone has a purpose, I think." said Praying Frog. "I just don't know mine."

Now the leader of the Council began the questioning.

"Is it not your purpose to be a productive member of your community?

"I think I am a productive member of my community, but I am not sure that is my purpose."

"Is it not your purpose to be the head of your family, and to love your wife and children?"

"I do lead and love my family with all my heart, but I am not sure that is my purpose."

"Is it not your purpose to be the best frog that you can be?"

"I have tried my entire life to be the best frog that I can be, in everything I do, but I am not sure that is my purpose."

"Is it not your purpose to perpetuate the values, traditions, and customs of your frog army and species?"

"Sir, I do all of those things on every chance I get, but I am not sure that is my true purpose in life."

"One moment, son, while the Council confers," he said to Praying Frog. The Council then circled up out of the earshot of Praying Frog and they croaked and croaked for quite some time before they determined the answer to Praying Frog's inquiry.

Meanwhile, Praying Frog waited patiently. He could see the Toads conferring, but he could not hear their words. He believed, in fact, he knew, that once they had determined his purpose, and advised him of it, he would start to live a better life, filled with meaning, living out his true purpose.

The Toad Council members conferred and conferenced on the question of Praying Frog's purpose for quite a long time. They bantered and queried each other and accessed the archives of their wisdom in search of a proper answer. Once the Toads had completed their conference they all turned to face Praying Frog to deliver their findings.

"Praying Frog, this Council has met and conferred on the question of your purpose. We have determined that we do not have the answer to the question you seek. It is beyond the scope of our knowledge and we can not help you."

Praying Frog felt all his joy and anticipation melt away as the Council member spoke. What would he do now? Would he end up just like the frog in his dream? "Thank you for your honesty, kind sirs. What should I do now?"

"There is one who can help you, if he is willing. He lives far from here. He is the oldest and wisest Bullfrog on the Earth. He is known as The Grandmaster and he is a very serious and frightening creature, but if there is anyone who knows the answer to your query it will be him."

"Where may I find this Grandmaster?" Praying Frog asked.

"One of our helpers will point you in the right direction, Praying Frog. Be careful, as the route is dangerous and long. Good luck finding your purpose in life."

With that, Praying Frog thanked the Council, once again, and departed from their presence. He rested for some time, in preparation for his journey. Once he awoke, one of the Council's helpers provided Praying Frog with some fresh flies, clean water, and a map to the location of the Grandmaster, keeper of the answer to his true purpose in life, and sent him on his way.

The Garter Snake

Praying Frog, then, anxiously started his journey for the Grandmaster's lair. While he knew the path would be long and dangerous he took comfort in the fact that, at the end of his journey, his purpose would be revealed. Joy and prosperity would, surely, follow.

He hopped through the night. He stopped, occasionally, to feed on flies and wet his skin, but he made tremendous strides in his journey in the hours of darkness. He thought it was best to travel in darkness, where he would be much less visible to his plentiful predators.

He started to reflect on his life and his accomplishments and deeds and started to feel sad and depressed. He was a beloved husband and the father of children he loved dearly. He was a productive member of his community. He always tried to help the members of his army, where he could, whether it was with physical chores, or sharing his, relative, wisdom, as one of the more educated members of the tribe.

He had always believed he was living a meaningful life. He thought he was living a life of purpose, integrity, and meaning. Then, in one instance, he discovered it was all meaningless. Why? Because he lacked a true purpose to his life. To Praying Frog, what had been revealed to him was that while he was doing good things in his life, he was doing them for no good reason, and with no real, directed goal in mind. Therefore, it was meaningless.

These realizations made Praying Frog spiral quickly into a deep depression. He was overcome with sadness, emptiness, and loneliness. His excitement rested in the fact that this state of meaninglessness would not last for long; it was not permanent. Once he reached the Grandmaster, and learned his true purpose, the days of sadness would be just a memory.

As the dawn broke over the horizon, Praying Frog was quickly approaching the place on the map identified as the home of the Grandmaster. His heart raced and he felt a sense of youthful vitality that he had not felt in so many years. Once he received the wisdom of the Grandmaster he would be reborn.

Praying Frog was so excited he did not observe the mature garter snake slithering along side him, tracing, carefully, his every step. The cunning snake was enjoying the chase. For this solitary creature enjoying the hunt was almost as enjoyable as the taste of the prey in his belly. This meal, an adult frog, would sustain him for some time. He was very excited.

Praying Frog was, normally, very aware of his environment and his surroundings. As a father and army elder, he was always on the lookout for predators in the protection of his family; however, now was a different time. Praying Frog had become so fixated on finding his purpose that he had become numb to some of the elements of the world he lived in. More importantly, he was so focused on finding his purpose that he neglected to be alert to surrounding danger, like the approaching garter snake.

After some time following Praying Frog, the garter snake decided the time had come to strike. He was becoming bored with the chase, and the promise that the frog would lead him to an army of frogs was waning, so he figured he would strike before some mishap let this meal get away.

The garter snake then picked up speed, passing Praying Frog on the right, without his knowledge, and then circled left, directly in the path of Praying Frog. Praying Frog was so distracted that he didn't even notice the garter snake until he almost hopped right into his open mouth.

"Oh dear," shouted Praying Frog, as he screeched to a halt, just in time. The saliva of the garter snake, alone, would have ended Praying Frog's journey, forever.

"Sssssssss…," the serpent uttered. "Where are you going in such a hurry, little frog?" asked the colorful viper.

Praying Frog recoiled and said nothing. He was paralyzed with fear. Why was this snake engaging him in common conversation?

"Go on, answer my question," urged the snake. "You seem so determined. I would love to know what is so urgent as to keep you from noticing me?"

"I am on an important mission," said Praying Frog, proudly but timidly.

"Sssss…You, a lowly frog, on an important mission. That is the funniest thing I have ever heard," said the snake. "Mission to do what?"

"Do you really want to know?"

"Yes, I wouldn't ask if I wasn't curious. Or I could just eat you now and get it over with. Doesn't matter to me."

"No, please wait.   I am on a mission to find my true purpose."

At this point the garter snake moved from a position where he was completely horizontal to one where his body was coiled and his head raised and perched, ready to strike Praying Frog in the blink of an eye.

"Your true purpose? What is it you are talking about?"

"My true purpose. I am on a journey to seek out my true purpose, so I may lead a life of meaning and value in fulfillment of it."

"Little frog," said the snake. "I have good news and bad news for you."

"You do?" Praying Frog asked, in great surprise.

"Yes, I do," uttered the snake. "I know your true purpose and I intend to reveal it to you."

Praying Frog was shocked.   He never expected his true purpose to be revealed by the enemy of his kind, a deadly, garter snake.

"Please kind snake, share my purpose with me.   I will be forever in your debt. I thought you were my enemy. I had you all wrong."

"Little frog. I hope you are ready to receive this information, and I hope it will offer value and meaning to your pitiful life."

Praying Frog was overcome with surprise and joy. He was about to learn his true purpose from the least likely party on the planet he expected to learn it from, a garter snake. His journey had not been in vain.

Then the snake spoke to him, "Your one true purpose in life, Praying Frog, is to be my food. That is all a lowly, common frog was created for, and now I intend to help you fulfill that noble purpose by devouring your flesh and digesting you in my belly." The snake was so amused with himself he could not contain his laughter.

Praying Frog could not believe he had fallen for the snake's trickery. He, actually, believed that the snake was about to bestow the wisdom upon him that he was seeking. He was so desperate to learn the answer to the question he sought, that he allowed all good sense to be dispensed with. Now he stood powerless and motionless, about to have his journey ended, his quest unfulfilled, in the belly of his predator.

Praying Frog closed his eyes and prepared to be eaten. While it seemed hopeless, all was not lost for the little frog. At the moment prior to the snake's rancid jaws closing around the body of Praying Frog, a Red-Tailed Hawk swooped down from the sky and grabbed the snake in his talons and flew off in the distance with the serpent dangling in the air.

When Praying Frog opened his eyes, the snake was gone. He wasn't sure, at first, if he was amidst a dream, or if he was awake; but when he gazed upon the coiled imprint of the garter in the ground before him, he knew it was not a dream.

More importantly, when he opened his eyes, he could see the habitat of the Grandmaster in the distance. This vision distracted him from his fear and disbelief over what had just occurred. He quickly cleared his thoughts and raced for the wisdom of the Grandmaster Bullfrog.

The Grandmaster

Praying Frog inched closer and closer to the log where the aged Bullfrog sat with his eyes closed. Gazing upon this elder behemoth, with his long white beard flowing, his weathered face, his stern look, his staff in hand, brought real fear to the heart of Praying Frog.

"Proceed no further," muttered the Kwanjangnim, or Grandmaster, as he came to be called. The Grandmaster was fully aware of the younger's presence. "Who dares disturb me?"

"I am Praying Frog, Master," he said, sheepishly. "I have journeyed far for an audience with you."

"WHY?" he demanded to know.

"I need you to teach me my purpose in life," Praying Frog prayed.

With this, the Bullfrog's face softened as his belly swelled, and he began to roar with laughter. "Is this really why you have come?"

"Yes Master."

"You have journeyed far?"

"Yes."

"You have left your family?"

"Yes."

"You have risked your life?"

"Yes, more than once."

"All so I that may show you your purpose in life?"

"Yes, Master, please. I am completely paralyzed without a sense of purpose. I cannot go on until I understand my purpose. I have been completely unable to function since I learned about my void of purpose."

"What will you do once I reveal your purpose to you?" the Bullfrog inquired.

"I will spend the rest of my days fulfilling it to the best of my ability," Praying Frog said earnestly.

"My son, I can not help you."

"But why Master," Praying Frog asked desperately. "Why do you refuse to help me? Am I unworthy? Have I displeased you?"

"No, my son. I did not say I was unwilling to help you. I said I was unable to."

Praying Frog began to become frantic, "I do not understand, Master. Have I traveled all this way for nothing? Has the journey been meaningless?"

"Praying Frog, the journey was anything but meaningless.

In fact, the journey was EVERYTHING. It was not the journey that is your problem, it is the premise upon which it was based."

"Tell me more, Master."

"Don't you see, my boy? Only you can discover your purpose, Praying Frog. Many frogs spend their entire lives seeking their purpose from others, as you have. They risk their lives, their fortunes, and their happiness in order to discover their purpose. They travel miles upon miles, as you have, seeking the wisdom of others, when the answer to this question lies right in front of them, and in front of you."

"Please go on," Praying Frog said. He was beginning to feel a sense of calm overcome him.

"The purpose of your life can only be found in one place and it is not here, in my presence, Praying Frog. Nor is it anywhere you have been along your journey."

"So, where Master? I will go there now."

"It is not a location, Praying Frog. Your purpose can only be found in your heart and in your mind. No one can define your purpose in life for you. You must discover it for yourself, within yourself."

"How will I know when I discover it, Master?"

"Our lives are a constant journey. You must proceed with honesty. You must be honest with yourself, first, and with others, always. You must act out of pure love, always. Always be true to the essence of your true nature, Praying Frog. You must look deeply in your heart and in your mind. You must obtain harmony with the universe, the physical and the spiritual."

The Grandmaster paused, and then he proceeded.

"When these things are true, when you are in harmony and tranquility with the universe, only then, when you least expect it, will your true purpose will be revealed to you."

"But how long will that take?"

"For every individual the timing is different. It isn't about time, my son; it is about your readiness to receive the message. For some, they are never ready and their purpose is never, truly, revealed to them. It is, entirely, dependent upon you. I do offer you this advice, Praying Frog. You must never allow your quest for purpose to make your life meaningless. Proceed with joy, with love, and with appreciation. If you do these things, regardless of whether you find out your purpose in life, your life will have great meaning."

"I understand, Master. Thank you."

"Now leave me, Praying Frog. I am old and I must rest now. Safe journey."

With that Praying Frog took leave of his great spiritual teacher and headed home to his family and his lily pad. For the first time since the Fly had spoken to him, Praying Frog felt a sense of genuine peace.

Conclusion

Praying Frog journeyed home, safely, to his beloved family and the army of his clan. He hugged and kissed them, with heartfelt appreciation upon his return. The children clamored for his affection and for the details of his dangerous journey. He shared some stories and reserved others, as he felt appropriate. He was genuinely pleased to be home, in the comfort of those he loved.

He spent the next days of his life following the advise of the wise, old Bullfrog. He lived, he loved, and he played. He was true to his self and true to others. He meditated often on the state of his life and of the world. He still sought his purpose daily, but he knew, with time and patience, it would be revealed to him. When the universe was ready to deliver it he would be ready to receive it.

He realized that the journey had taught him so much. While he sought the definitive answer to his purpose in life, he learned that if, while seeking to discover our true purpose we sacrifice of all the things that have value in our lives, in search of that purpose, we deprive our lives of any meaning and value, whatsoever.

No one can tell us our purpose. We must discover it for ourselves. We cannot force that discovery. We will uncover that purpose when we have laid the proper foundation and the time is right. Until that time, life is meant to be, joyfully, lived out to the fullest. Take joy in every step of the journey.

Made in the USA
Middletown, DE
19 November 2020